kratts' CREATURES ™

In Search of the REAL Tasmanian Devil

by James Preller

SCHOLASTIC INC.

New York   Toronto   London   Auckland   Sydney

Photo Credits:
Exclusive worldwide licensing agent: Momentum Partners, Inc., New York, NY
All graphic maps: Lisa Kelly
Cover: All photos © 1996 Paragon Entertainment Corporation.
Interior: p. 3-6 © 1996 Paragon Entertainment Corporation; **p. 7** (top left and bottom right) © 1996 Paragon Entertainment Corporation; (bottom left) © TomMcHugh/Photo Researchers, Inc.; **p. 8** All photos © Dave Watts/A.N.T. Photo Library; **p. 9** © Fredy Mercay/A.N.T. Photo Library; **p. 10** (left) © 1996 Paragon Entertainment Corporation; (center) © Gerard Lacz/Peter Arnold, Inc.; (right) © Tom McHugh/Photo Researchers, Inc.; **p. 11** (top) © Tom McHugh/Photo Researchers, Inc. (bottom left) © TomMcHugh/Photo Resarchers, Inc.; (bottom right) © Ronald Seitre/Peter Arnold, Inc.; **p. 12** (left) © R. van Nostrand/Photo Researchers, Inc. (right) © Mike James/Photo Researchers, Inc.; **p. 13** © 1996 Paragon Entertainment Corporation; **p. 14** © 1996 Paragon Entertainment Corporation; **p. 15** (left) © 1996 Paragon Entertainment Corporation; (right) Painting by Diane Green © Dave Watts/A.N.T. Photo Library; **p. 16** All photos © 1996 Paragon Entertainment Corporation; **p. 17** (top left and top right) © 1996 Paragon Entertainment Corporation; (bottom left) © Erwin and Peggy Bauer/Bruce Coleman Inc.; (bottom right) © Steve Kaufman/Peter Arnold, Inc.; **pp. 18-19** All photos © 1996 Paragon Entertainment Corporation; **p. 20** Eric Robertson/ © 1996 Paragon Entertainment Corporation; **pp. 21-24** © 1996 Paragon Entertainment Corporation; p. 25 © John Cancalosi/Peter Arnold, Inc.; **p. 26** (top) © H. Reinhard/Okapia; (bottom) © Zig Leszcynski/Animals Animals; **p. 27** (top left) © Tom McHugh/Photo Researchers, Inc.; (bottom left) © D. & V. Blagden/A.N.T. Photo Library; (top right) © Joyce Photographics/Photo Researchers, Inc.; (bottom right) © 1996 Paragon Entertainment Corporation; **p. 28** © Fredy Mercay/A.N.T. Photo Library; **p. 29** (left) © Jack Cameron/A.N.T. Photo Library; (right) © Michael Dick/Animals Animals; **p. 31** (top row) © 1996 Paragon Entertainment Corporation; (left center) © Tom McHugh/Photo Researchers, Inc.; (bottom row) © 1996 Paragon Entertainment Corporation; **p. 32** © 1996 Paragon Entertainment Corporation.

ISBN 0-590-53739-3

Book design by Todd Lefelt

12 11 10 9 8 7 6 5 4 3 2 1   6 7 8 9/9 0 1/0

Printed in the U.S.A.   2 3

First Scholastic printing, October 1996

Hi! I'm Chris Kratt.

And I'm Martin Kratt!

We're going to Tasmania in search of the real, live Tasmanian devil! Do you want to come along? Turn the page and let the adventure begin!

FunFact #1

The Tasmanian devil lives in only one place on earth, a mysterious island called, oddly enough, Tasmania!

This is Tasmania.

That's weird. It looks like a map to me.

Australia

Tasmania

Very funny! It's a map of Tasmania—an island off the southern coast of Australia.

Tasmania is really amazing. It's got a beautiful coastline, incredible mountains, eucalyptus trees, and really thick rain forests. We're going to start our search in the eucalyptus forest.

All kinds of wild and crazy things have been said about the Tasmanian devil. People who believe the cartoons on TV think the Tasmanian devil twirls around super-fast and buzzes through trees. And that's not all. Some folks say Tasmanian devils are vicious hunters that attack sheep in packs of 20 or more!

But before we believed stories like that, we checked it out for ourselves.

Fun Fact #2

You know how in cartoons the Tasmanian devil spins like a whirling top? Well, that's almost true for the real Tazzy as well. When facing an enemy, the Tasmanian devil takes two poses—a side view to make itself appear larger, and then a front view, which shows off its fierce teeth. By quickly switching these positions, the devil kind of looks as though it is spinning around.

Wombat

Cool! Let's meet the creatures!

Hey guys! Ttark here in Tasmania. This place is wild.

Platypus

Kookaburra

Some of my best friends are hopping, crawling, swimming, and climbing around here! Platypuses! Wombats! Kookaburras! There are creatures everywhere....

Ttark's right! This incredible island is filled with tons of far-out animals! So let's take a break from our Tazzy search to check out one of my personal favorites! Let's face it. The platypus is one of the weirdest-looking creatures in the world! It has a bill and feet like a duck, a tail like a beaver, fur like an otter, and venom like a rattlesnake. It also lays eggs—like a bird!

Creature Feature
Platypus

Tail like a beaver!

Bill like a duck!

Once hunted by humans for its velvetlike fur, the platypus is now protected by law. It can be found in the freshwater of eastern Australia, from North Queensland to Tasmania.

Venom like a rattlesnake!

Feet like a duck!

The platypus is a great underwater swimmer. It paddles with its front feet, steers with its back feet, and—believe it or not—keeps its eyes closed!

Platypuses like the nightlife. They rest all day in tight burrows along the water's edge. At night, they are active—swimming, feeding, and playing in the water.

Spur

The platypus's venom is in spurs on its hind legs.

Like most mammals in and around Australia, Tasmanian devils are marsupials. That means they are in the same family as kangaroos and koalas.

Kangaroo

Koala

For now, we've got to stick to our Tasmanian devil search. But we hope to be back to look at these guys someday soon.

Like many marsupials, a Tasmanian devil baby is born blind, deaf, and hairless. It is only one quarter of an inch long. When it is born, it must feel and smell its way from the birth canal to the nipple in its mother's pouch.

I'm checking out what it might feel like to be a newborn Tasmanian devil!

I've met some crazy creatures in my day, but this one takes the cake!

13

FUN FACT #3

The Tasmanian devil has 42 teeth, perfect for slashing, ripping, grinding, and crushing. The Tasmanian devil is too clumsy and slow to be a good hunter, so it eats animals that have already been killed or died. And it eats everything—hair, skin, flesh, bones, and teeth!

Tasmanian devils have one of the strongest bites of all animals. When it comes to biting, they are right up there with hyenas and sharks.

Hi guys! **Allison** here, from the Creature Club. While you're out there searching for the Tasmanian devil, keep your eyes peeled for another animal—the Tasmanian tiger. The last known one died in the Hobart Zoo in Tasmania back in 1936. I'm just hoping that somewhere in that forest are a few Tasmanian tigers no one has spotted.

WHAT KILLED OFF THE TASMANIAN TIGER?

Tasmanian tigers sometimes killed sheep. This made the sheep farmers angry, and soon, the sheep farmers began killing Tasmanian tigers. In 1888, to get rid of the Tasmanian tiger population, the Tasmanian government actually offered money to anyone who killed one! The plan worked too well. Now we don't think there are any Tasmanian tigers left alive at all!

You guys are halfway through the book and you still haven't found a Tasmanian devil. Don't you have a plan or something?

Don't we always?

Chris and Martin's Five Easy Steps to Finding a Tasmanian Devil

1. Find a dead wombat! Or, hey, a dead anything.

2. Wait until night falls.

3. Sit in the dark and wait for  sniffy sounds.

4. When you hear noisy grunts, growls, and screams, then you know there's an eating frenzy and...

5. Turn on your flashlight and watch the Tasmanian devil chow down!

Creature Feature
Wombat

Check this out. I was searching for a Tasmanian devil, and look what I discovered! It's a wombat!

● Wombats look like little bears. Their average weight is about 60 pounds. They have terrible eyesight, but great hearing and good noses. They prefer spending time in the dark.

● Wombats like to eat grass. And more grass. And more grass. And then, for a change, more grass!

● Wombats live in underground tunnels called burrows. Their short legs and sharp claws are perfect for digging. When you've got that, who needs shovels?

That wasn't our stomachs making those loud, creepy, horrible howls and wails. **That's a...**

Yyyyyooooowwiiii!

Growwwiii!

Grrrr!

Tazzy devil!

FUN FaCt #4

During the day, Tasmanian devils usually sleep in hollow logs, caves, or old burrows. Then, as the sun goes down, the jet-black Tazzy devil comes out to seach for food.

Dear reader, we now interrupt this very serious and wildly exciting moment for two pages of complete silliness...

WARNING: Trust us, dear reader. If a Tasmanian devil ever asks you over for dinner, be prepared to get really sick. Tasmanian devils eat rotten junk that a human body could never digest. You'd probably get sick just smelling the stuff they think is delicious.

Yowgrrowkerryaa!

A GUIDE TO TASMANIAN DEVIL MANNERS

Make disgusting, slobbering noises as you eat. Gulp down food as fast as you can. Eat until you are very full. Then eat lots more. Don't talk with your mouth full. Instead,

SCREAM! GRUNT! HISS! SNARL! SNARL!

In other words, eat like your friends at the school cafeteria.

Tasmanian devils can really pack it away! It's normal for a Tasmanian devil to eat about one third its weight—in an hour! That's like a 60-pound fourth-grader eating 80 quarter-pound hamburgers for lunch!

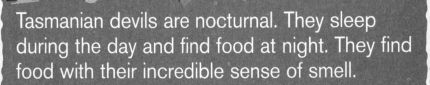

FunFact #5

Tasmanian devils are nocturnal. They sleep during the day and find food at night. They find food with their incredible sense of smell.

Is this the ugliest animal on earth?

The verdict: He's so ugly, He's kind of cute!

FunFact #6

Tasmanian devils gather around meals in a wild feeding frenzy, just like sharks do. Tough and agressive, these little devils often fight over food. The hungriest devil usually wins!

Tasmanian devils once lived all over Australia, but today you won't find a single one. One of the reasons is because of the dingo, a wild dog of Australia that just loves to munch on Tasmanian devils. The Tasmanian devils just could not compete with these fierce, wild dogs. Fortunately for the Tasmanian devil, dingos never came to live on Tasmania. That sure made life easier for the T-devils.

Dingo

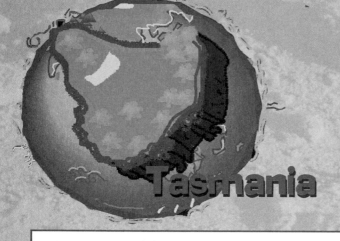
Tasmania

Here are a few other animals we saw in Tasmania (but couldn't fit into the book in any other way).

The very cute but wildly ferocious tiger quoll. It's actually in the same family as the Tasmanian devil and the Tasmanian tiger.

The slow-moving
ring-tailed possum

The poisonous tiger snake

The echidna

And this other weird-looking
creature with goggle-eyes.
Whoops! That's Martin wearing
night vision goggles!

Creature Feature
Kookaburra

If you are in Tasmania and you hear somebody laughing, you might be near a kookaburra. But that's not laughter at all. It's just the way the kookaburra marks its territory. Think of it as putting a fence around your yard. The kookaburras just do it with a song.

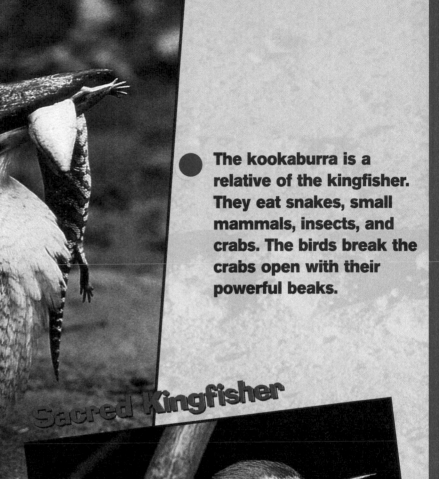

The kookaburra is a relative of the kingfisher. They eat snakes, small mammals, insects, and crabs. The birds break the crabs open with their powerful beaks.

Sacred Kingfisher

Hey guys! I just got some good news. The word from the hill country is that there may have been a sighting of a Tasmanian tiger. No one seems to know for sure. Let's hope!

We'll keep hoping Ttark. Unfortunately, we've probably lost the Tasmanian tiger forever. We're just lucky the Tasmanian devil didn't meet a similar fate. And not just because we like them. These devils are really important animals.

They aren't mean ferocious killers after all. We like to think of Tasmanian devils as nature's best recyclers. They clean up the countryside of animals that have already died, and that is good for everybody.

We've reached the end of our adventure.

You mean because we've finally learned the truth about Tasmanian devils?

Yes, but also because... WE'VE RUN OUT OF PAGES!